LIBRARY
D0931326

INVISIBLE WORLDS

Inside the Human Body

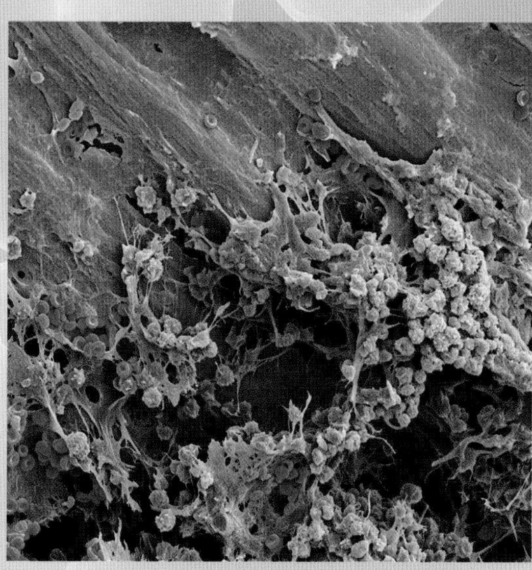

Jolyon Goddard

New York

Published by Marshall Cavendish Benchmark
An imprint of Marshall Cavendish Corporation

Website: www.marshallcavendish.us

Other Marshall Cavendish Offices:
Marshall Cavendish International (Asia) Private Limited, 1 New Industrial Road, Singapore 536196 • Marshall Cavendish International (Thailand) Co Ltd. 253 Asoke, 12th Flr, Sukhumvit 21 Road, Klongtoey Nua, Wattana, Bangkok 10110, Thailand • Marshall Cavendish (Malaysia) Sdn Bhd, Times Subang, Lot 46, Subang Hi-Tech Industrial Park, Batu Tiga, 40000 Shah Alam, Selangor Darul Ehsan, Malaysia

Library of Congress Cataloging-in-Publication Data
Goddard, Jolyon.
Inside the human body / by Jolyon Goddard.
p. cm. — (Invisible worlds)
"Describes the fascinating details of the human body that are too small for the unaided eye to see,
and how these microscopic systems work to keep the body alive and healthy"—Provided by publisher.
Includes bibliographical references and index.
ISBN 978-0-7614-4190-8
1. Body, Human—Juvenile literature. 2. Human physiology—Juvenile literature. I. Title.
QP37.G64 2010
612—dc22
2008037254

Series created by The Brown Reference Group
www.brownreference.com

For The Brown Reference Group:
Editor: Leon Gray
Designer: Joan Curtis
Picture Managers: Sophie Mortimer and Clare Newman
Picture Researcher: Sean Hannaway
Illustrator: MW Digital Graphics
Managing Editor: Miranda Smith
Design Manager: David Poole
Editorial Director: Lindsey Lowe
Children's Publisher: Anne O'Daly

Consultant: Dr. Nicholas Jenkins

Front Cover: Science Photo Library: Steve Gschmeissner; inset: Shutterstock

The photographs in this book are used by permission and through the courtesy of:
Science Photo Library: 38; Dr Tony Brain: 42; Thomas Deerinck NCMIR: 21 (bottom); Eye of Science: 7, 22, 25, 27, 31, 41; Dr Robert Friedland: 44; Steve Gschmeissner: 1, 14, 17, 23 (top), 32, 33 (bottom), 35 (left), 43 (bottom); C. J. Guerin, PhD, MRC Toxicology Unit: 19, David McCarthy: 4–5; Susumu Nishinaga: 13, 37; D. Phillips: 8; K. R. Porter: 29 (bottom); ISM Sovereign: 20, 34; Geoff Tompkinson: 11; Zephyr: 28; Shutterstock: Dario Sabljak: 10.

Printed in Malaysia (T)
1 3 5 6 4 2

Contents

Introducing the Human Body

The human body is a living machine. **Cells** are its microscopic building blocks. By the time you have read this sentence, 50,000 cells in your body will have died and been replaced with new cells. Cells group together to form **tissues**, which hold the body together.

The body's **organs** are the biggest parts of the machine. The organs work together to ensure the body stays healthy. The brain is an organ that tells other organs what to do. For example, the brain keeps the heart pumping blood around the body. The brain also takes in information from the senses and sends messages to muscles to make them move. The brain sends and receives these instructions through a network of billions of nerve cells that stretch throughout the body.

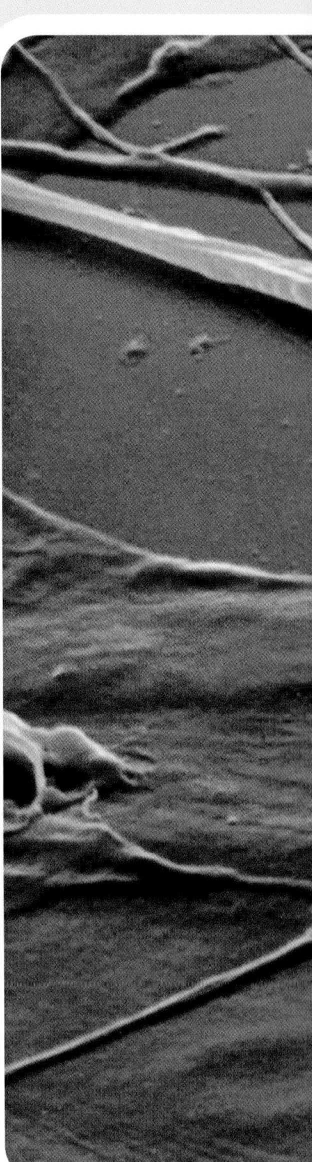

This is a nerve cell from part of the brain called the cerebellum. The brain is the control center of the body.

CHAPTER 1

Body Works

The human body is made up of many different parts. The smallest units are called cells, and they are incredibly small. About 500 average-sized body cells would cover the period at the end of this sentence. Cells that do similar jobs group to form tissues such as bone or muscle. In turn, tissues combine to make the major body organs, such as the brain and heart.

The cells, organs, and tissues that share the same jobs work as body systems. So all the parts that work together to help people breathe—parts include the diaphragm, lungs, and trachea (windpipe)—are known as the respiratory system. The digestive system includes all the cells, tissues, and organs involved in breaking down food. These include the gallbladder, liver, pancreas, and stomach. The bones, joints, and **ligaments** are together called the skeletal system. All the muscles, including the muscles found in the heart, work as part of the muscular system. Other systems include the circulatory system (the heart, blood, and the vessels that carry blood), the nervous system (brain, nerves, spinal cord, and sense organs), and the urinary system (bladder, kidneys, ureters, and urethra).

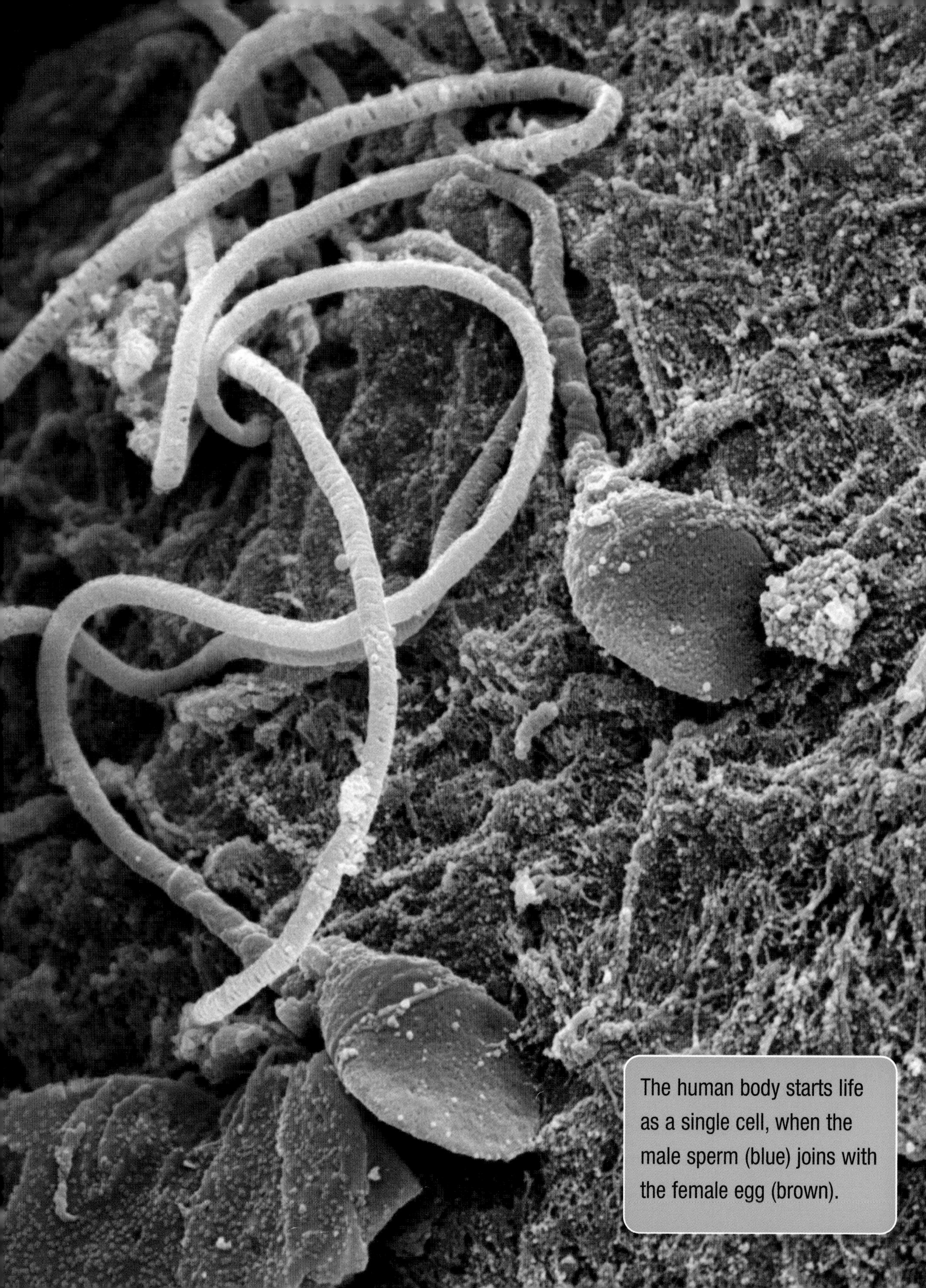

The human body starts life as a single cell, when the male sperm (blue) joins with the female egg (brown).

Cells and Tissues

Trillions of cells make up the human body. They come in many different shapes and sizes. The shape of a cell may reveal what job it does. A nerve cell passes messages around the body, so it has many long branches. A muscle cell is long and thin to stretch and contract, or shorten, as it moves.

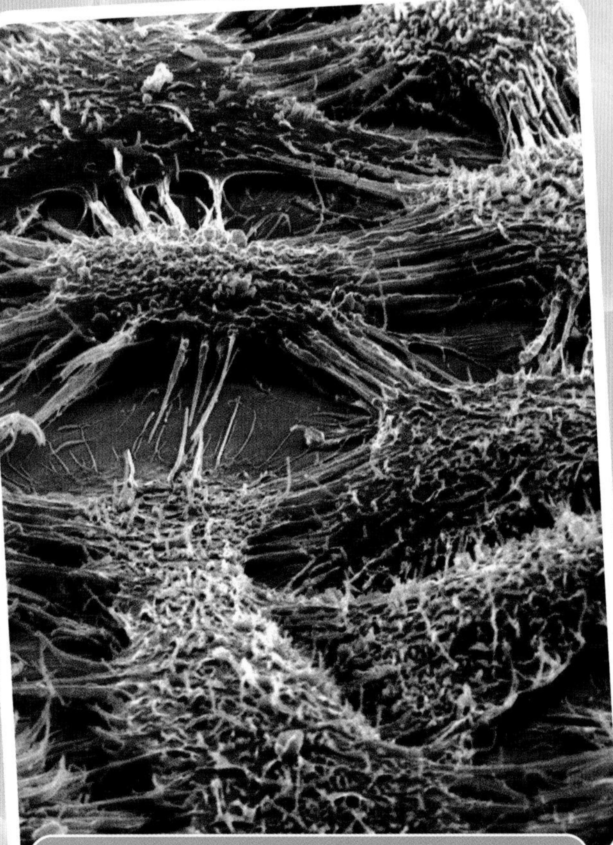

Tiny skin cells can only be seen under a powerful microscope.

Building the body

Cells are the building blocks of tissues. The cells in specific tissues have similar shapes and sizes, and they all do a particular job. Some cells and tissues group to form organs. For example, the liver is an organ made up of epithelial cells, connective tissue, nerve cells, and the liver tissue. And the brain is made up of connective tissue and epithelial cells, and nerve cells.

Inside cells

Each cell has its own tiny organs called **organelles**. These include the Golgi body, ribosomes, mitochondria (the singular form is mitochondrion), and the endoplasmic reticulum. Each organelle does a specific job within the cell. The Golgi body packages **proteins** that will be released by the cell when needed. Ribosomes help make proteins. The endoplasmic reticulum helps to carry proteins inside the cell. Mitochondria produce energy to do all these jobs. Organelles float around in a watery fluid called cytoplasm. A layer of fat, called the cell membrane, encloses the cell. The membrane allows only certain substances in and out of the cell.

Command center

The nucleus is the command center of the cell. It contains instructions, called **genes**, that control how cells, tissues, organs, and the body develop, grow, and work.

Inside a typical human cell are many organelles such as the Golgi body, mitochondria, ribosomes, and the endoplasmic reticulum.

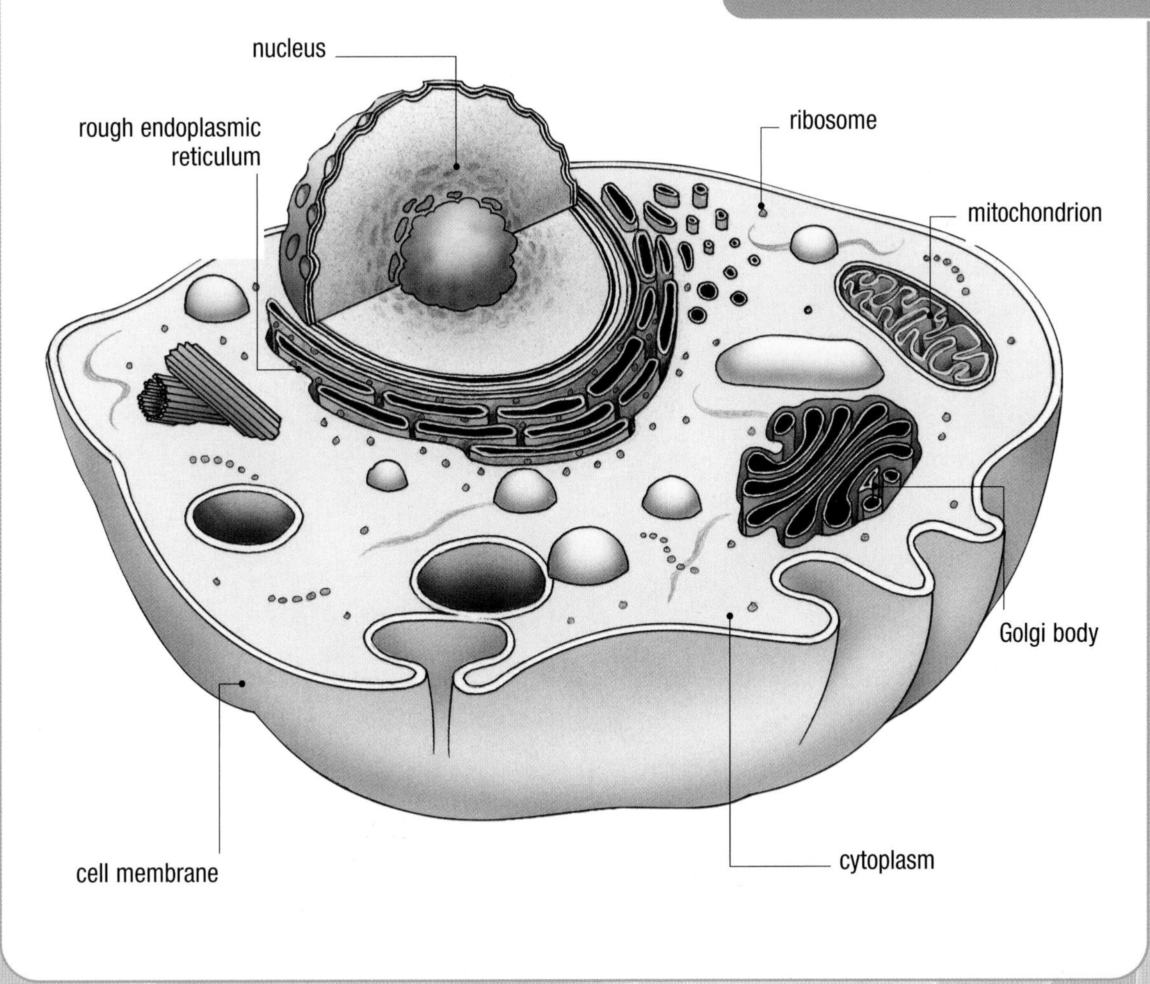

Look Inside

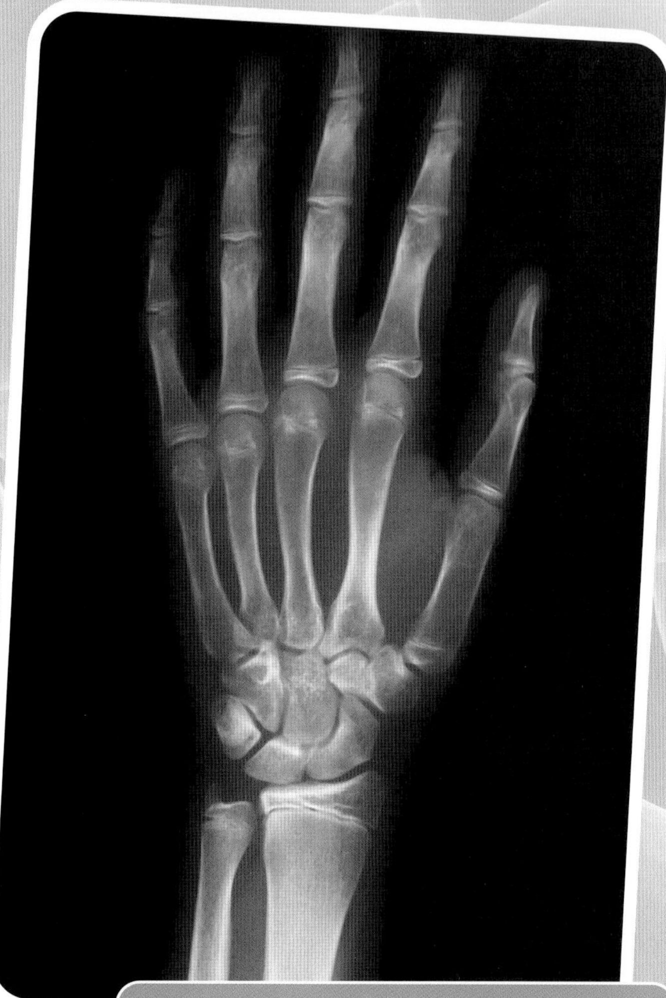

This X ray clearly shows the bones inside the hand.

Cells are so tiny that people use microscopes to see them. Light microscopes use light rays and lenses to magnify cells up to 2,000 times their original size. Even more powerful microscopes use electrons to see tiny objects. Electrons are small particles found inside atoms. Electron microscopes bounce beams of electrons off cells and other tiny objects to produce three-dimensional pictures. The images may be several million times the size of the object in view.

Medical imaging

When someone is ill, a doctor may need to look inside the patient's body. Doctors commonly use X rays to do this. X rays are waves of electromagnetic radiation, just like visible light. An X-ray picture forms on photographic film. X rays can pass through soft tissue, such as skin. Hard tissue, such as bone, blocks the rays. So the X rays that hit the film turn it black, but because bone blocks the X rays it is seen as white on the image.

Another way to look inside the body is to use an endoscope. This flexible viewing tube can be inserted into the body through an opening like the mouth. There is a light and tiny camera on the end of the endoscope so the surgeon can see details on a monitor.

Did You Know?

Technicians use high-frequency sound waves called ultrasound to look inside the body. The waves bounce off the insides of the body and can be used to form an image. Ultrasound is often used to check on babies before they are born.

Computer imaging

Computers can create very clear pictures of the body. In CT (computed tomography) scans, a computer uses a series of X rays to build up a three-dimensional picture of tissues and organs in the body. Magnetic resonance imaging (MRI) uses magnets, radio waves, and computers to make pictures of soft body tissues. MRI scans produce pictures of body parts that do not show up well in X rays or CT scans, such as **cartilage** in joints.

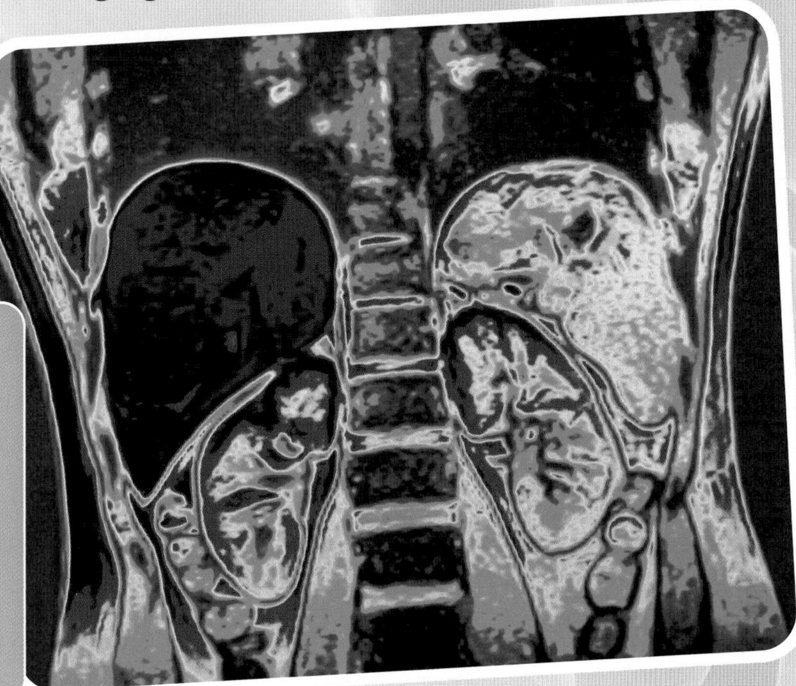

A MRI scan shows the kidneys on both sides of the spine (the bony structure in the center). The liver is the darker organ above the kidney on the left of this picture.

CHAPTER 2

Made for Movement

Bones and muscles are hidden away underneath the skin. Bone and muscle might be invisible but they do an important job. They work together to help people move around.

The skeleton is the collective name for all the bones in the body. The skeleton makes up 20 percent of the body's total weight. Bones are tough and hard and give people their human shape. Bones meet at joints, and they connect to each other by ligaments. Like any other part of the body, bone is living tissue. It is continually being renewed. The body replaces the skeleton in about seven years. Minerals such as calcium and phosphorus are locked away inside bones. These minerals give the bone its great strength. They can also be released if the rest of the body needs them. Soft tissue called marrow fills the center of a bone. This is the site of blood cell production.

Muscles are the "meat" of the body. They form layers under the skin and attach to bones by tough, fibrous tissues called tendons. Muscles help the body to move. They contract, or shorten, pulling on the bones. Muscles usually work in pairs, contracting and then relaxing to make the body move.

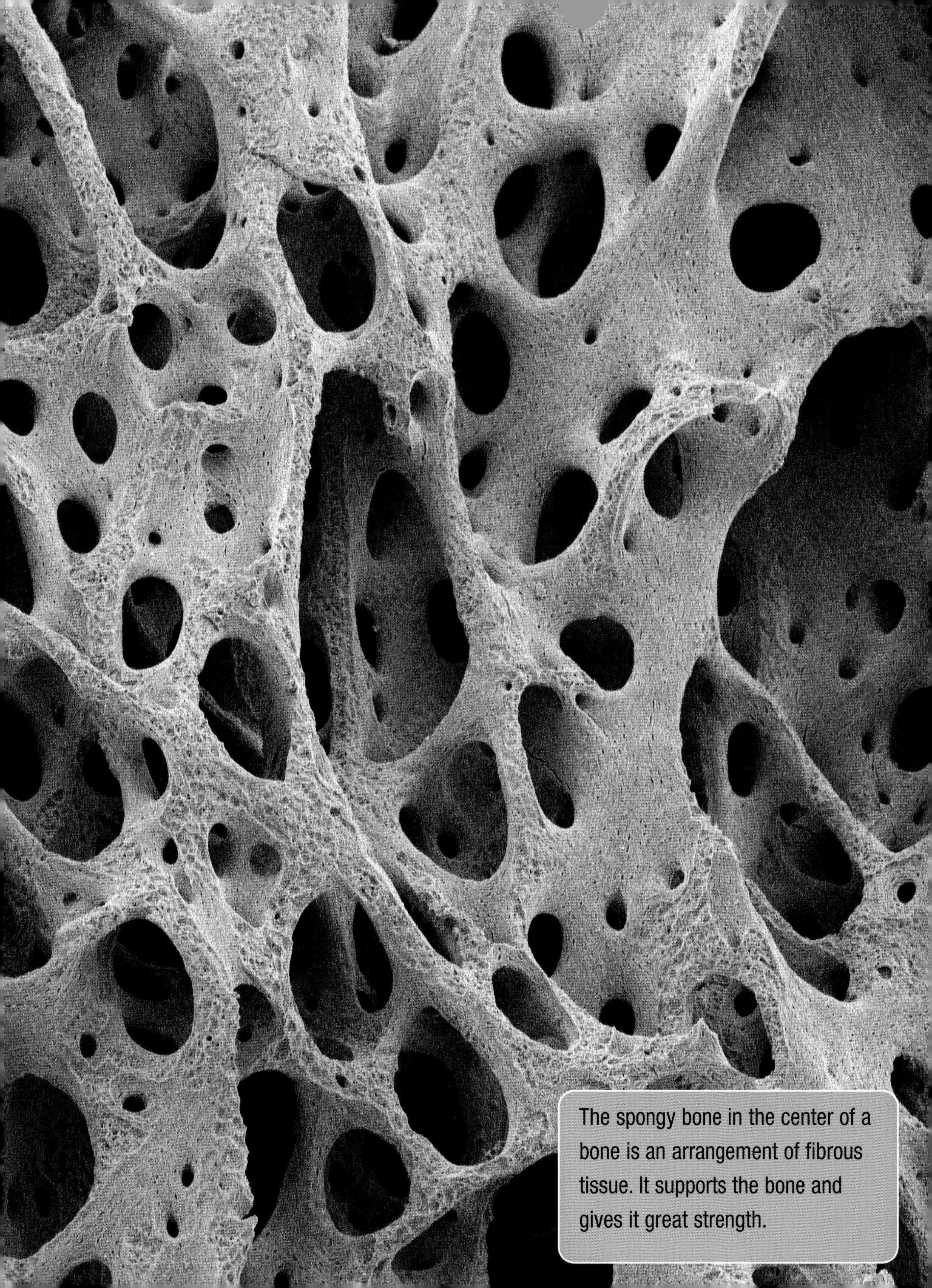

The spongy bone in the center of a bone is an arrangement of fibrous tissue. It supports the bone and gives it great strength.

Bones and Joints

Bones come in different shapes and sizes. Long bones, such as those in the legs, act as levers and help the body move. Other bones protect organs. The skull protects the brain. The ribs enclose the heart and lungs.

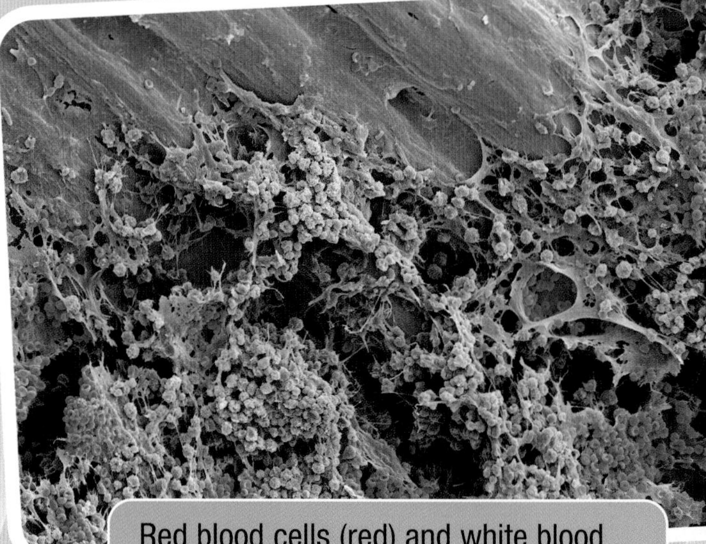

Red blood cells (red) and white blood cells (orange) are made by the marrow inside a bone.

Inside bones

A typical bone is made up of several layers. The thin outer layer is called the periosteum. Beneath the periosteum is a layer of hard, compact bone. This layer gives the bone its strength. It consists of bundles of rod-shaped cells called **osteons**. Beneath the compact bone is a layer of spongy bone. This layer has an arrangement of fibrous tissue that looks like a bath sponge. Fibrous tissue is a mass of white collagen fibers joined by connective tissue. Spongy bone is strong, but it is much lighter than compact bone.

Within the gaps of the spongy bone and in the bone's center is soft tissue called marrow. There are two

Fast Facts

- A human adult has about 206 bones in his or her body.
- Babies are born with about 350 soft bones in their body. The soft bones join together as the child grows.

Did You Know?

Many joints are surrounded by a capsule. The inner lining of the capsule, called the synovial membrane, produces a liquid, called synovial fluid. This "oils" the ends of the bones, so they slide over each other smoothly when they move. These joints are called synovial joints.

different types of marrow. Red marrow produces the main blood cells—red and white blood cells and platelets. In some of the bones, red marrow eventually stops making blood cells. When this happens, it turns into a fatty tissue called yellow marrow.

Blood vessels run throughout the bones, supplying the living tissue with oxygen and **nutrients**.

Meeting place

A thin tissue layer, called cartilage, covers the ends of bones at joints, cushioning the bones from damage. Ligaments are tough strips of tissue that connect bones to joints. There are different kinds of joints. Some are fixed and do not move, for example, where the bones of the skull meet. These joints are called sutures. Others are flexible, as in the ball-and-socket joints at the hips.

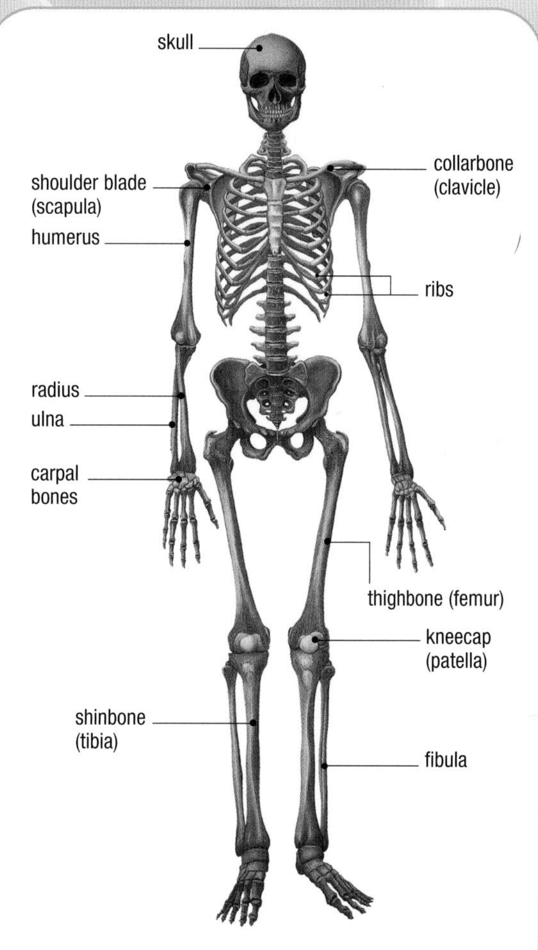

The adult skeleton is made up of 206 different bones that support the body and protect the soft internal organs.

Muscle Power

Muscles make up about two-fifths of the body's weight. The biggest muscles are the two glutei maximi, which make up the buttocks, and the latissimi dorsi, which move the arms and shoulder. Muscles in the face give people expressions such as a frown or a smile. It takes forty muscles to make a frown. Smiling uses only seventeen muscles.

Different muscles

There are three different types of muscles. Skeletal muscles attach to the bones and help the body to move. There are about 650 of these skeletal muscles in the body. The heart is another type of muscle. Heart muscle is continuously contracting and relaxing. This allows blood to be pumped throughout the body.

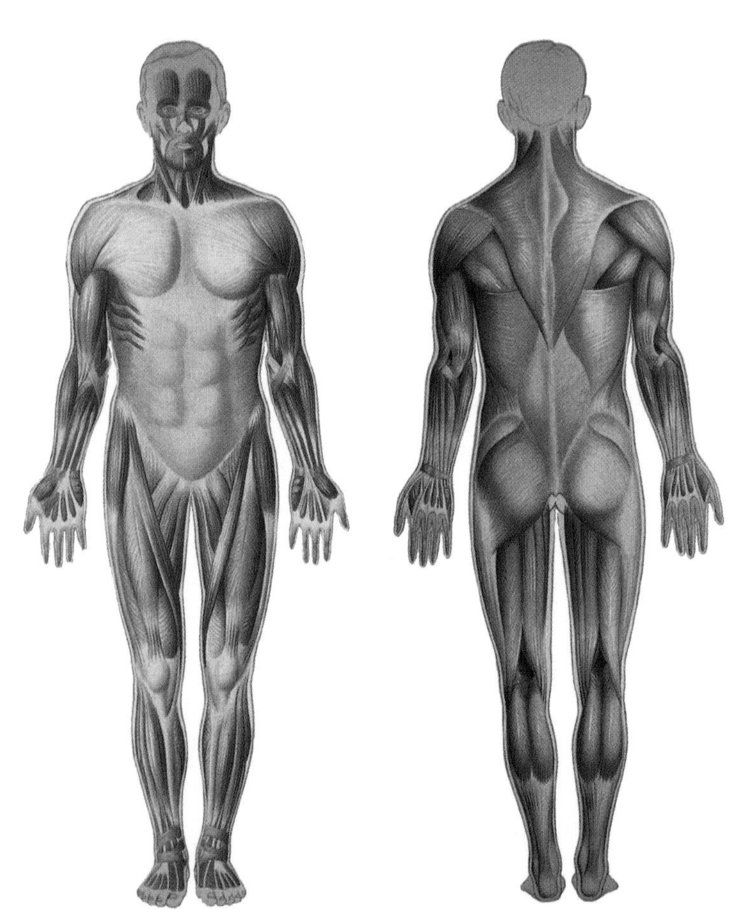

These illustrations show the main skeletal muscles in the body. Skeletal muscles control movements such as bending and running.

When viewed under a powerful microscope, skeletal muscle has a pattern of stripes. These are the myofibrils in the muscle fiber.

Smooth muscle is found in the walls of the digestive tract and blood vessels.

Muscle fibers

Skeletal muscle consists of bundles of long muscle fibers. These fibers can contract rapidly and powerfully, but only for short periods of time. Muscle fibers are made up of smaller fibers called myofibrils, which line up in a regular pattern to form a muscle fiber. In turn, the myofibrils are made up of even smaller fibers called myofilaments. The thin myofilaments are mainly made up of strands of a protein called actin. Thicker myofilaments are mainly made up of strands of a protein called myosin.

Close Up

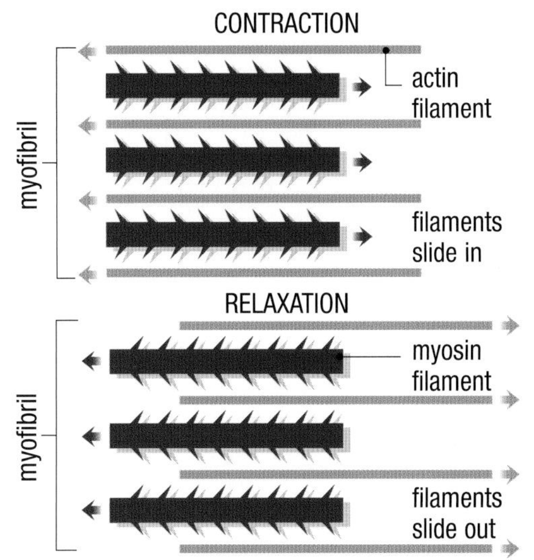

Muscles contract when they receive a signal from the nervous system. When the muscle contracts, the myosin filaments slide in between the actin filaments. This shortens the myofibrils and the muscle. When the muscle relaxes, the actin and myosin filaments slide out. In this state of relaxation, the actin filaments only partially overlap with the myosin filaments, making the myofibril and the muscle longer.

CHAPTER 3

Brain and Senses

The brain is a mass of more than 100 billion nerve cells called **neurons**. The brain sits inside a protective case called the skull. From there, the brain controls everything that happens inside the body. Many of the things that the brain does happen without people thinking about them. They include activities such as breathing and sweating. The brain also allows people to plan, think, speak, be creative, and have emotions. All of these complex brain processes are probably the result of different parts of the brain working together to think and imagine things.

The brain is the center of the nervous system. It connects to the spinal cord, which runs through the center of the bony spine. Together, the brain and spinal cord are known as the central nervous system. They connect to a large network of nerve fibers (bundles of neurons) inside the body. The fibers send messages as electrical signals. Information returns to the brain along sensory nerves. For example, the optic nerve delivers information from the eye to the brain. Motor nerves, such as the sciatic nerves that run down each leg, carry signals back from the brain to the muscles.

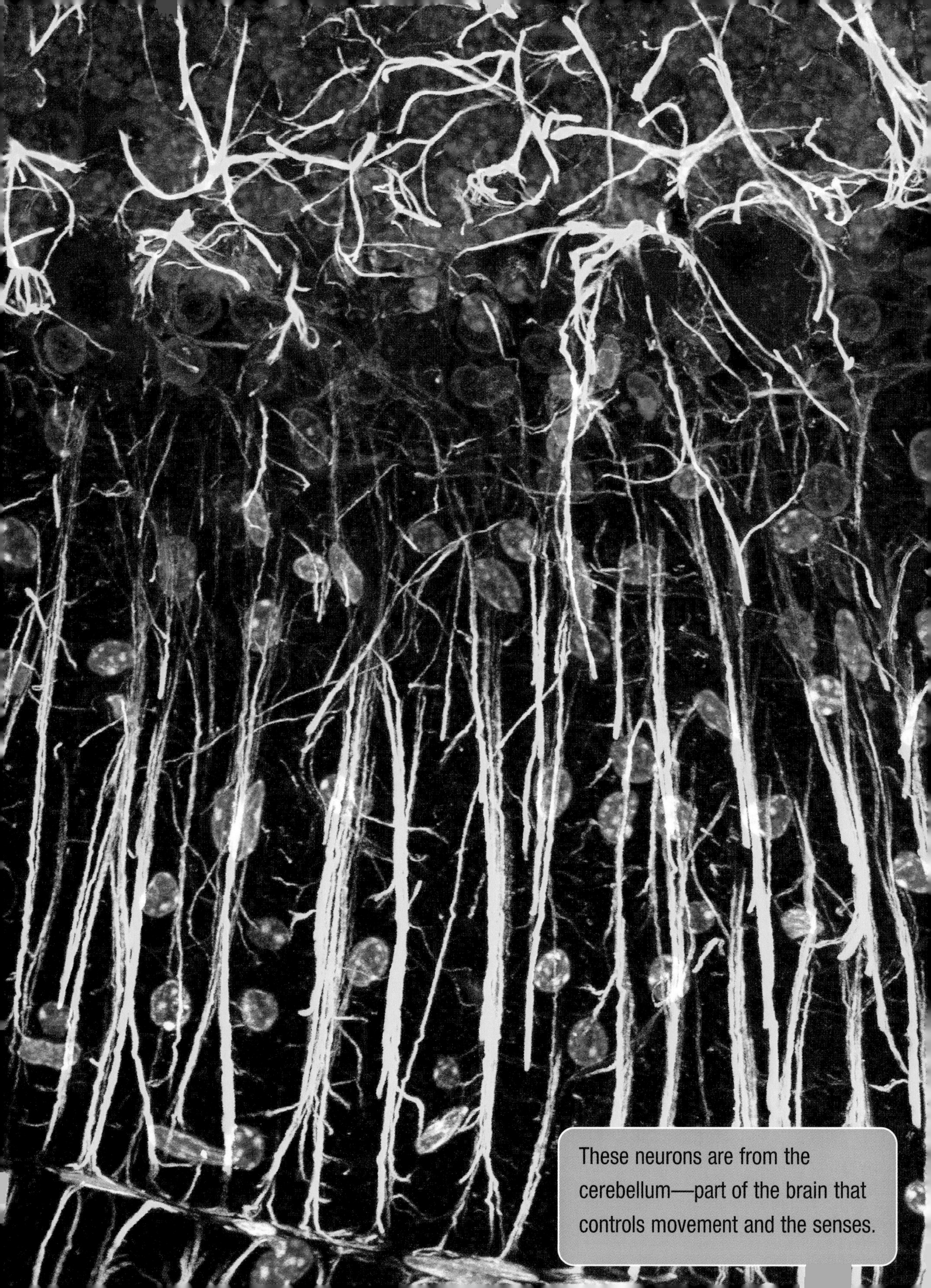

These neurons are from the cerebellum—part of the brain that controls movement and the senses.

Nerves and the Brain

The nervous system is made up of billions of incredibly small neurons. A typical neuron consists of a cell body, which contains the nucleus, and a long fiber called an **axon**, which carries the electrical signals. The cell body usually has many spiky projections, called **dendrites**, which stick to other neurons. Many axons group together inside a fatty layer of myelin. This insulates the neurons, speeding up the electrical signals as they pass along the axon.

For a nerve signal to pass from neuron to neuron, it has to cross a gap called a **synapse**. Electrical signals cannot jump this gap.

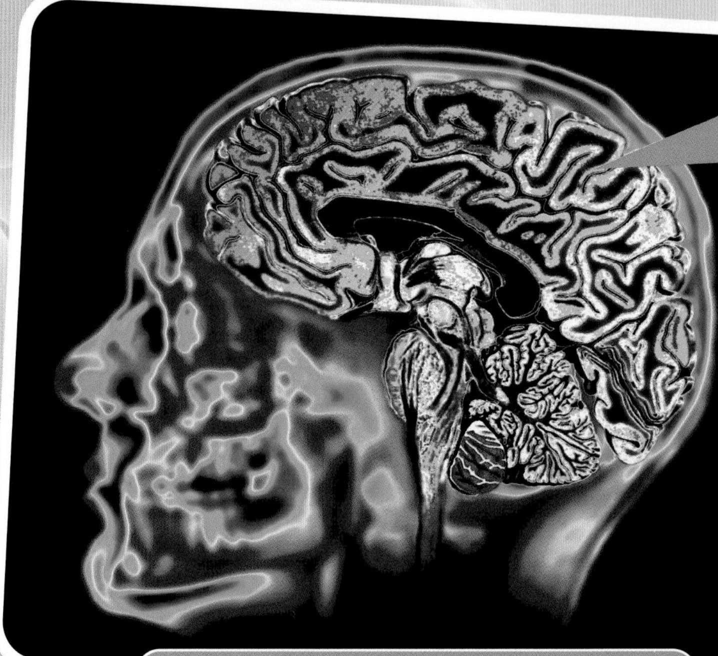

Magnetic resonance imaging reveals folds of the cerebral cortex. This is the outermost layer of the cerebrum, which is the largest part of the human brain.

Fast Facts

- Nerve signals travel at about 180 miles (290 km) per hour.
- The brain stops growing in size when you are fifteen years old.
- About 20 percent of the body's blood is directed to the brain because it needs a lot of oxygen and nutrients to work.

Close Up

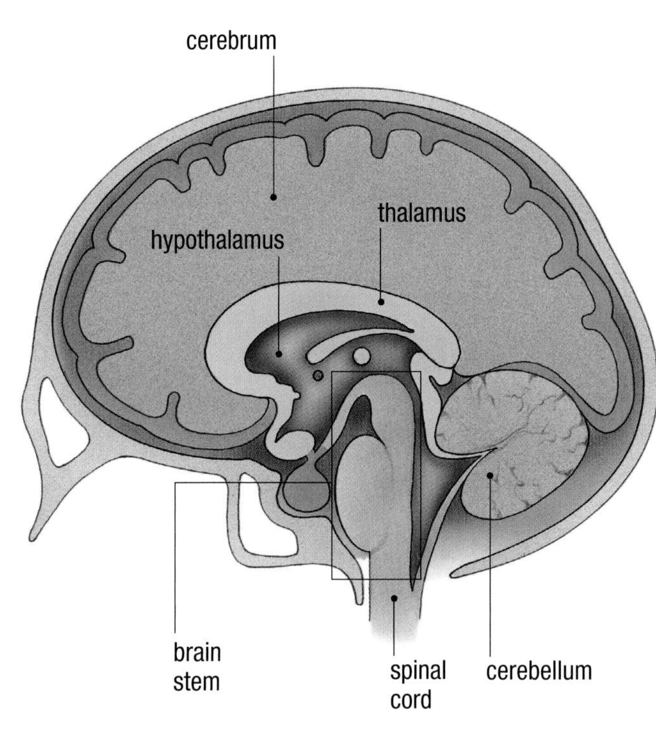

Different parts of the brain do different jobs. The cerebrum is the main part of the brain. The cerebrum processes complex information. The cerebellum controls balance and body movements. The hypothalamus controls body temperature, hunger, and pain. The thalamus relays messages between the brain stem and the cerebrum. The brain stem controls breathing and heart rate and relays messages from the brain to the spinal cord.

Instead, they turn into chemical signals and then back into electrical signals in the next neuron. Neurotransmitters transmit chemical messages between neurons.

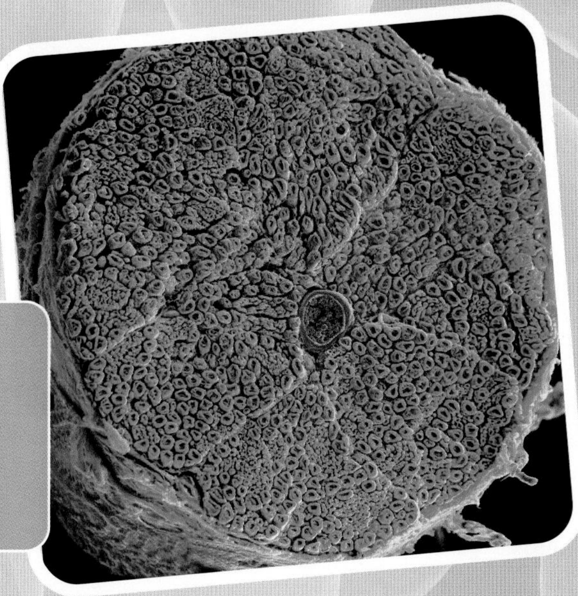

This cross-section of a nerve fiber shows a bundle of axons (green and blue) insulated inside a layer of fatty myelin. A blood vessel (pink) is shown in the center of the nerve.

Sensing the World

There are five main senses: hearing, sight, smell, touch, and taste. These senses pick up information from the outside world and pass it onto the brain. The brain then decides how to respond. This could result in a person walking over to something that looks interesting or listening to someone more carefully.

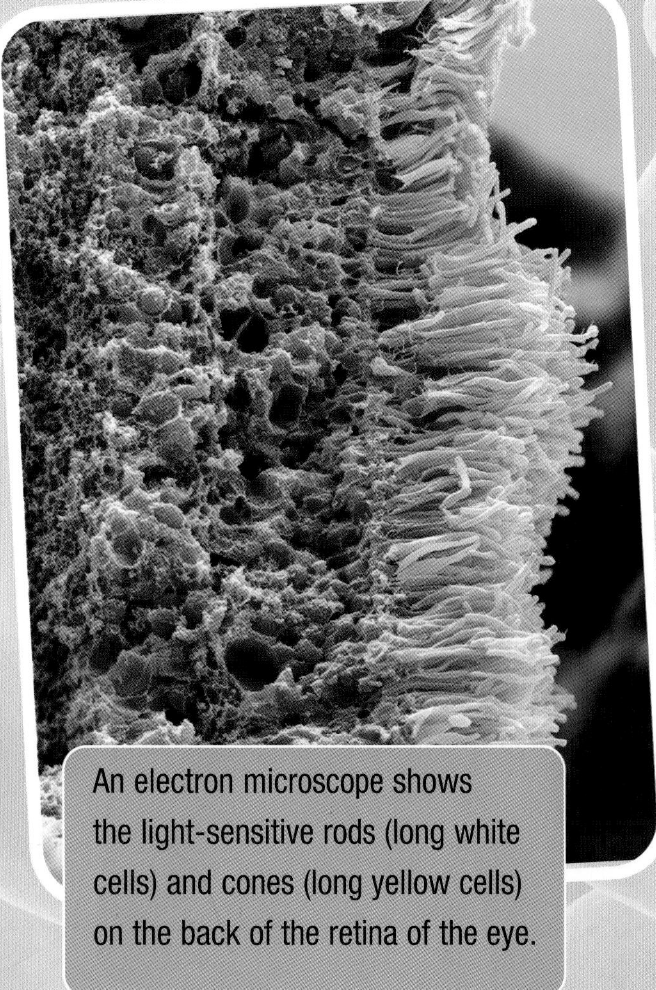

An electron microscope shows the light-sensitive rods (long white cells) and cones (long yellow cells) on the back of the retina of the eye.

Sense of sight

Eyes are the organs of sight. Light rays enter the eyes through tiny openings called pupils. The light then forms an image on the light-sensitive tissue, called the **retina**, at the back of each eye. The retina is packed with sensory cells called rods and cones. Each retina contains around 120 million rods. These cells help people to see at night or in dim light. There are about 6.5 million cones in the retina. They help people see in color.

When light strikes the rods and cones, the cells turn the image into electrical signals. These travel to the brain through optic nerves, which turn the signals back into an image.

Other senses

Many other sensory receptors send information to the brain so that people can interact with the world around them. There are hairs inside the ears that are involved in hearing. In the skin, there are receptors that respond to heat, pressure, touch, pain, and vibrations. Receptors in the roof of the nasal cavity, or nose, can detect more than 10,000 different odors. The upper surface of the tongue is covered with around 10,000 taste buds.

Close Up

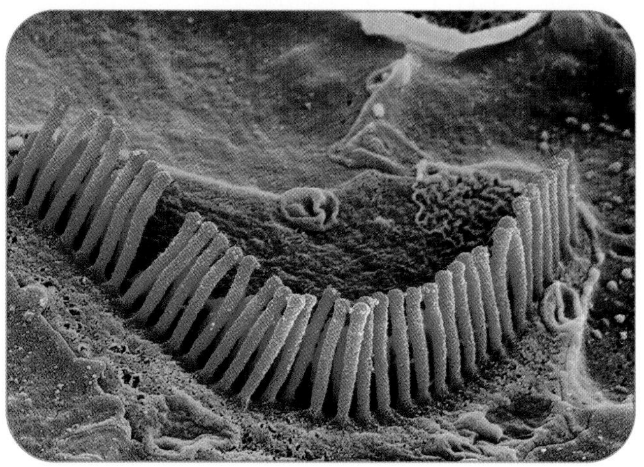

Sensory hair cells (red) deep inside the ear detect sound waves that pass into the ear. The hair cells turn the vibrations into electrical signals, which pass along the cochlear nerve into the brain for processing. Structures inside the ear also help us keep our balance.

Sound passes from the outer ear, into the middle ear and inner ear, and onto the brain through the cochlear nerve.

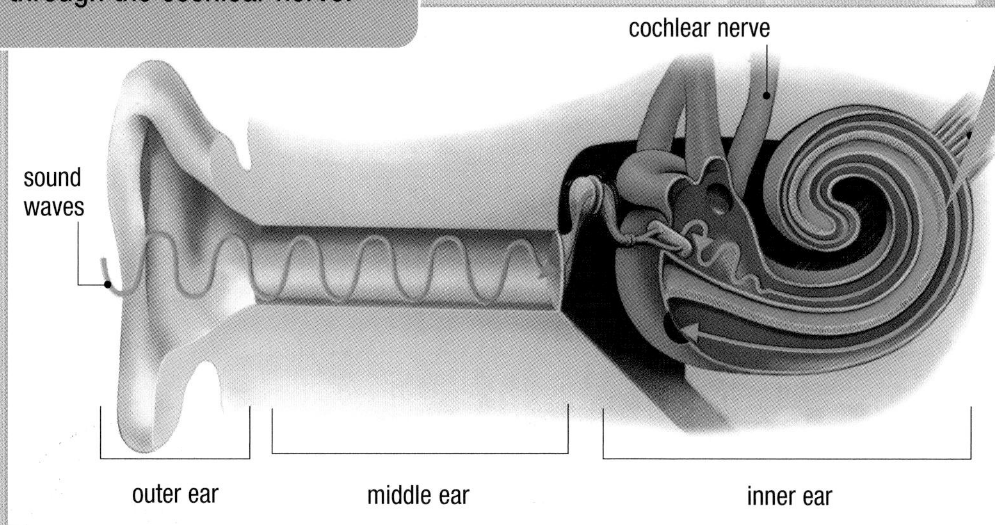

CHAPTER 4

Circulation and Breathing

Cells need food and oxygen to stay healthy. People breathe in oxygen all the time. It enters the body through the mouth and nose. The air passes into a network of fine tubes, called bronchioles, in the lungs. The oxygen ends up in tiny sacs, called **alveoli**, deep inside the lungs. There, the oxygen crosses the thin walls of the alveoli into tiny blood vessels, where it is picked up by red blood cells.

The oxygen-rich blood travels through blood vessels to an amazing muscular pump called the heart. Every day, the heart pumps around 2,500 gallons (9,450 liters) of blood around the body.

All the cells, tissues, and organs involved in breathing are known as the respiratory system. All the cells, tissues, and organs involved in blood transport are together called the cardiovascular system.

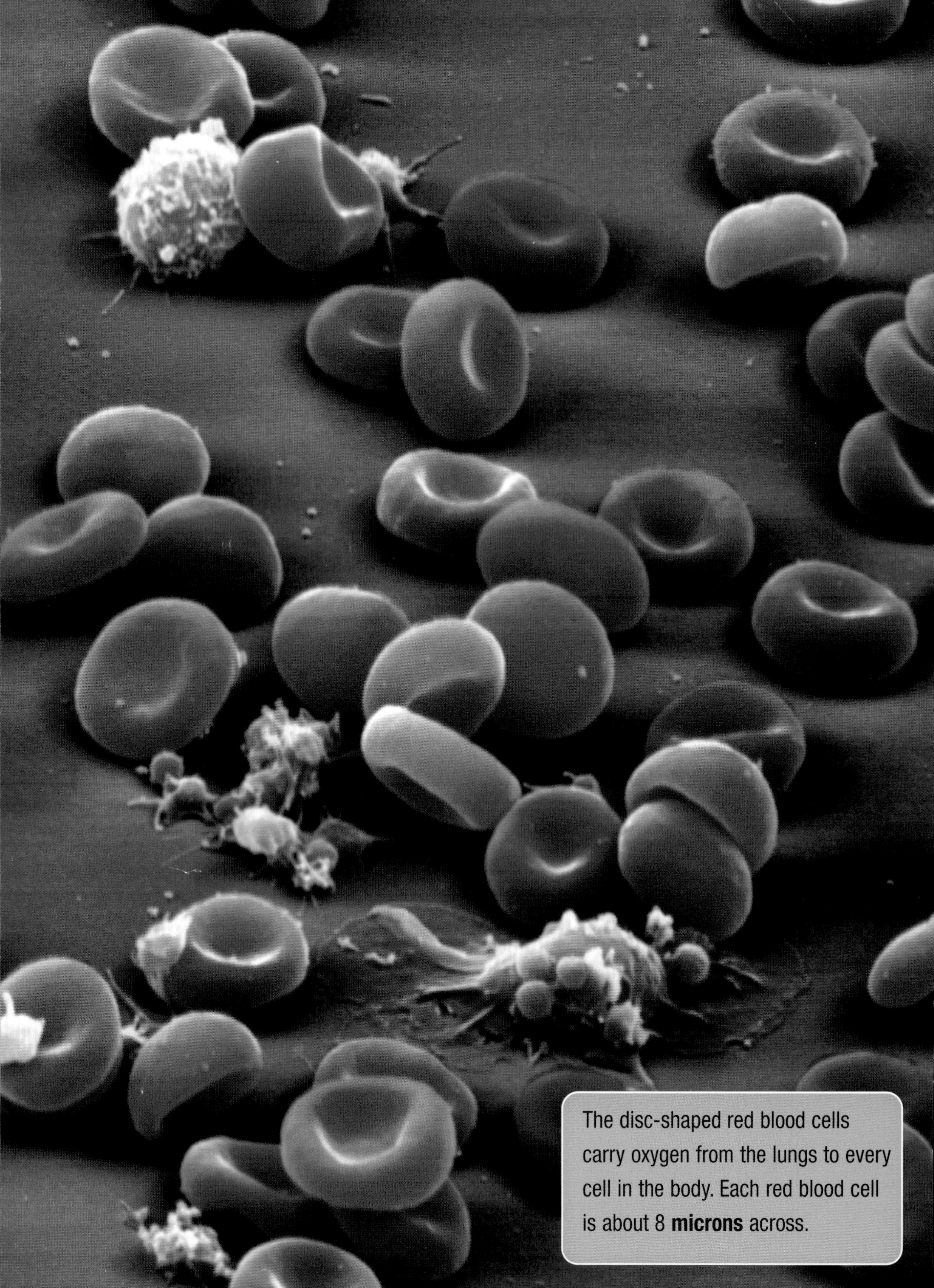

The disc-shaped red blood cells carry oxygen from the lungs to every cell in the body. Each red blood cell is about 8 **microns** across.

Blood Pump

The heart is an amazing organ. It is made from cardiac muscle. A healthy heart can work constantly without tiring. It beats about 100,000 times each day. Since the heart is working all the time, it uses up a lot of energy. So the cells that make up the heart are packed with energy-producing organelles called mitochondria.

Did You Know?

A healthy adult heart beats between 60 and 80 times every minute. During exercise it can beat twice as fast. Electrical signals controlled by the brain keep the heart beating.

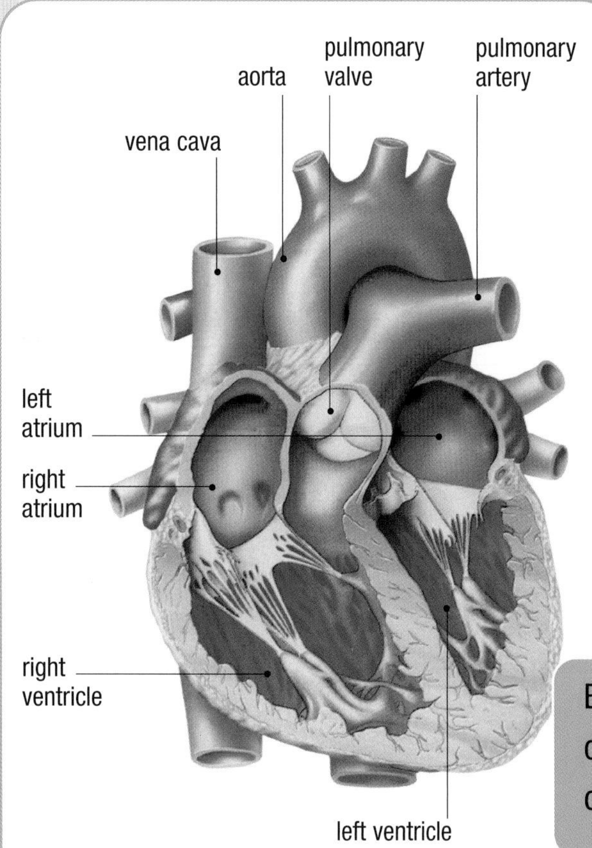

Inside the heart

An adult heart is about the same size as the adult's clenched fist. It is made up of four chambers. The two upper chambers are called atria (singular form is atrium). The two

Blood flows from the atria to the ventricles and out to the body. Valves between the chambers of the heart stop it from flowing backward.

lower chambers are called ventricles. The left and right sides of the heart are separated by a thick wall. This stops the blood in the two sides of heart from mixing.

Oxygen-rich blood from the lungs flows through the left atrium into the left ventricle and out to the body. Oxygen-poor blood from the body flows through the right atrium into the right ventricle and back to the lungs for more oxygen.

This capillary is so narrow that only a single blood cell can pass through it.

Blood vessels

Different blood vessels do different jobs. **Arteries** have thick, muscular walls and carry oxygen-rich blood from the heart to all the body's cells. **Veins** have thin, elastic walls and return oxygen-poor blood to the heart. Arteries divide into arterioles and veins into venules. Arterioles and venules connect by even thinner vessels called **capillaries**. Oxygen and nutrients pass through the thin walls of capillaries into cells. Waste substances, such as carbon dioxide, pass from the cells back into the blood and eventually out of the body.

The heart needs a lot of energy to keep beating. So its tissues need a good supply of oxygen and a sugar called glucose. The heart cannot get oxygen and glucose from the blood inside it. Instead, blood vessels around the heart supply the hard-working muscle with the nutrients it needs. These vessels are called coronary arteries and veins.

Breathing Air

People breathe air in through the mouth or nose. The air then passes down the throat and through a tube called the trachea (windpipe). The body has two lungs, so the trachea divides into two branches called bronchi (singular form is bronchus). One bronchus supplies the left lung with air. The other bronchus supplies the right lung. Deep within the lungs, each bronchus branches into thinner tubes. The thinnest tubes are the terminal bronchioles, and there about 30,000 of them in each lung. The ends of these bronchioles are surrounded by tiny air sacs called alveoli (singular form is alveolus).

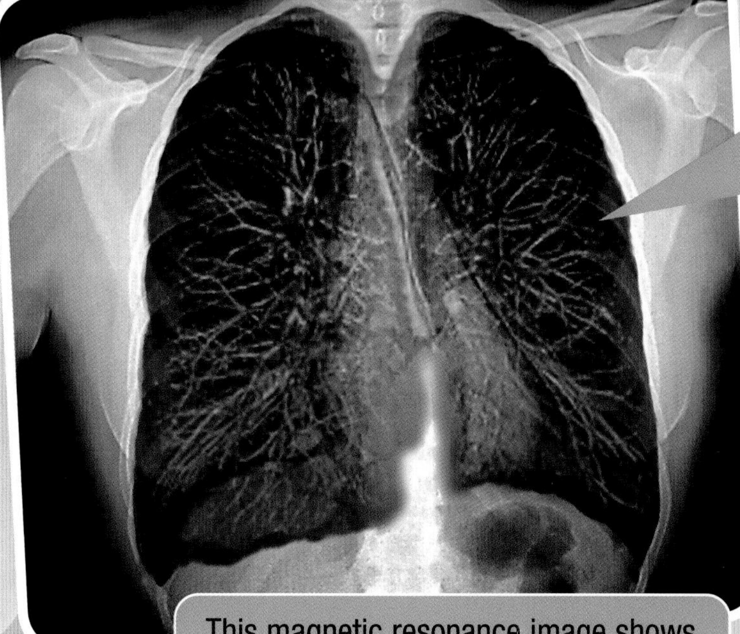

This magnetic resonance image shows the network of fine bronchioles that make up the lungs.

? Did You Know?

Without enough oxygen, cells cannot produce as much energy and do not survive for long. If glucose is not available, the body can break down protein and fats to make energy.

Inside cells

When oxygen arrives at a cell, it reacts with glucose. The reaction releases energy. This process is

Close Up

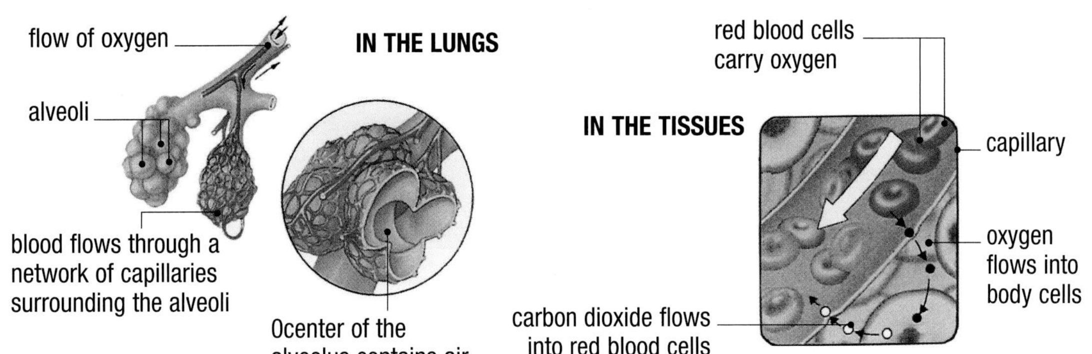

There are more than 300 million alveoli in the lungs. Each alveolus is tiny with very thin walls. They are arranged in clumps that look like bunches of grapes. A network of capillaries surround each clump of alveoli. Oxygen-poor blood passes through the capillaries, picks up oxygen in the alveoli, and takes it to the heart to be pumped around the body. Red blood cells carry the oxygen. The oxygen binds to a chemical called **hemoglobin** in the red blood cells. The hemoglobin gives up its oxygen when the red blood cells arrive at the tissues that need it.

called cellular respiration. It takes place in the mitochondria inside the body's cells. The energy produced by cellular respiration drives all the other reactions inside the body.

Cellular respiration has waste products—water and a gas called carbon dioxide. Red blood cells carry carbon dioxide back to the lungs. The carbon dioxide then passes through the capillaries into the alveoli so it can be breathed out.

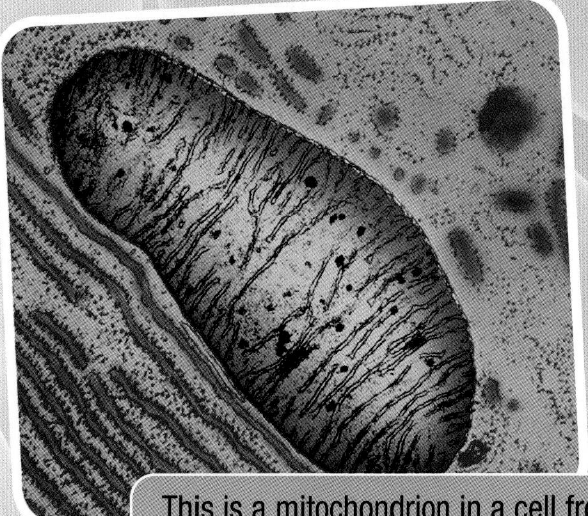

This is a mitochondrion in a cell from the pancreas. It is about 10 microns long.

CHAPTER 5

Processing Food

People need food for energy. The useful parts in food are called nutrients. They include fats, proteins, and **carbohydrates**. To be useful, nutrients have to be broken down into smaller molecules so they can be absorbed into the blood.

All the cells, tissues, and organs that make up the digestive system work to release the nutrients from food. The digestive system consists of the digestive tract, which is a long, muscular tube that runs from the mouth to the anus. Other parts include the gallbladder, large and small intestines, liver, pancreas, salivary glands, and the stomach.

The stomach is a sac that stores food while it is being digested. Food can spend up to five hours in the stomach. The stomach's muscular wall mixes and pushes the food around to break it down. The lining of the stomach makes acidic juices. Stomach acid breaks down food and kills any germs in it. The acid is strong enough to burn the skin. A layer of mucus (slime) lines the stomach and protects it from harm. Food passes from the stomach into the intestines, where nutrients enter the bloodstream. Waste products continue along the digestive tract and pass out of the anus as feces.

The lining of the stomach is called the mucosa. It consists of tiny cells that produce mucus to protect the stomach from digestive acids.

Eating Food

Digestion begins in the mouth. Teeth bite and chew food, breaking it up into smaller pieces. Three pairs of salivary glands release a watery liquid, called saliva, into the mouth. Saliva makes food wet. It also contains a protein called an **enzyme**. The enzyme reacts with carbohydrates in the food, breaking the molecules down into smaller substances. The tongue helps to mold the food into a ball, called a bolus, before it is swallowed. At the same time, the airway closes at the back of the throat so that food does not enter it and choke the person who is eating. The bolus passes the throat and into a muscular food tube called the esophagus, before entering the stomach.

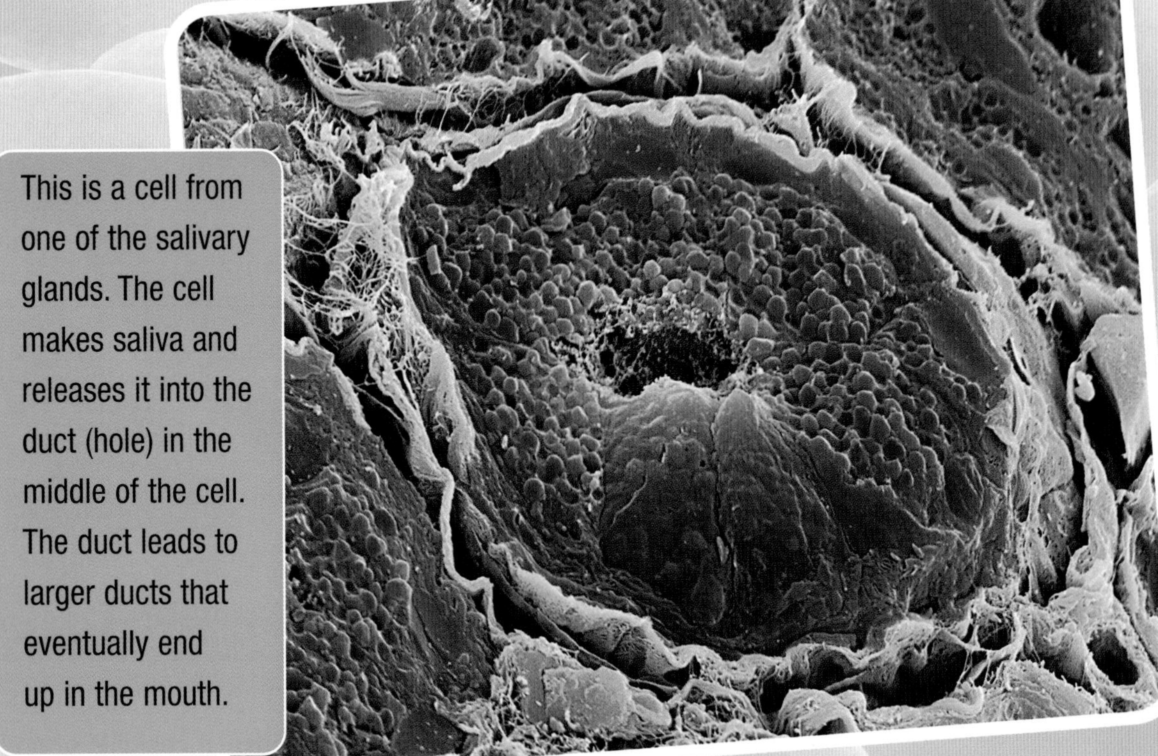

This is a cell from one of the salivary glands. The cell makes saliva and releases it into the duct (hole) in the middle of the cell. The duct leads to larger ducts that eventually end up in the mouth.

Peristalsis

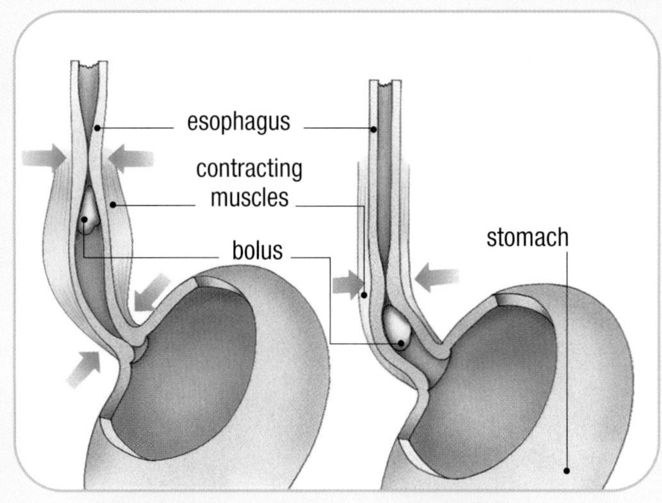

Waves of muscular contractions, called **peristalsis**, squeeze the the soft ball of food along the esophagus. Muscles in the wall of the esophagus contract and then relax, helping to push the food along until it eventually reaches the stomach. Peristalsis can be likened to squeezing toothpaste out of a tube.

You are what you eat

The main nutrients in food are called carbohydrates, fats, and proteins. To get the energy from these nutrients, they have to be broken down into molecules small enough to pass through the wall of the intestines. As the carbohydrates, fats, and proteins pass through the digestive system, enzymes help to break them down. Enzymes break down carbohydrates into simple sugars, proteins into amino acids, and fats into fatty acids and a chemical called glycerol.

Tiny ridges on the inner surface of the esophagus help push the food along.

Digesting Food

Inside the stomach, food mixes with more enzymes and acids that help break it down. The liquid food, called chyme, is then squirted into the intestines. Further digestion takes place in the small intestine. **Bile** salts made by the liver and stored in the gallbladder help break down fats. Enzymes produced by the pancreas and the wall of the small intestine break down the nutrients. These can then pass across the lining of the intestine and into the blood. From there, they travel to the liver for further processing.

Fast Facts

- In an average lifetime, a person eats about 65,000 pounds (30,000 kg) of food.
- The digestive tract of an adult is about 24 feet (7 m) long from beginning to end.

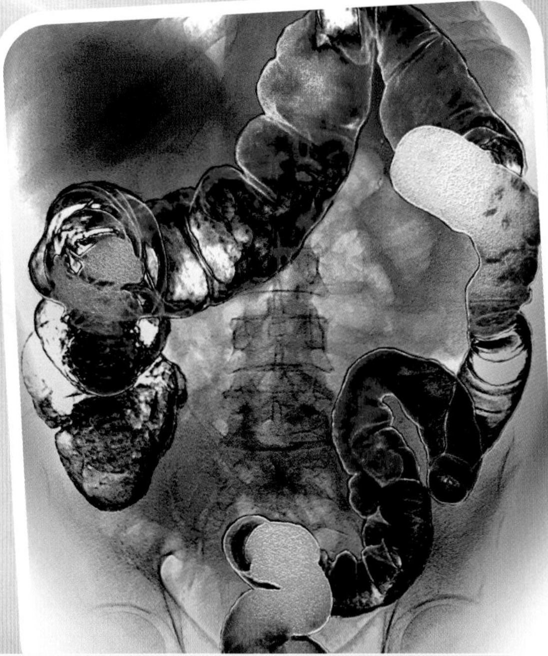

A colored X ray reveals a healthy colon (blue), which is the end of the digestive tract and leads to the anus. The colon absorbs water from undigested food.

Inside the liver

The liver does more than 250 jobs that break down, create, and store all kinds of substances. All these processes occur inside separate parts called lobules. Each lobule is supplied with arteries, veins, and

The small intestine is lined with tiny projections called villi.

bile ducts, which are channels that collect bile from the liver and deliver it to the intestines.

Close Up

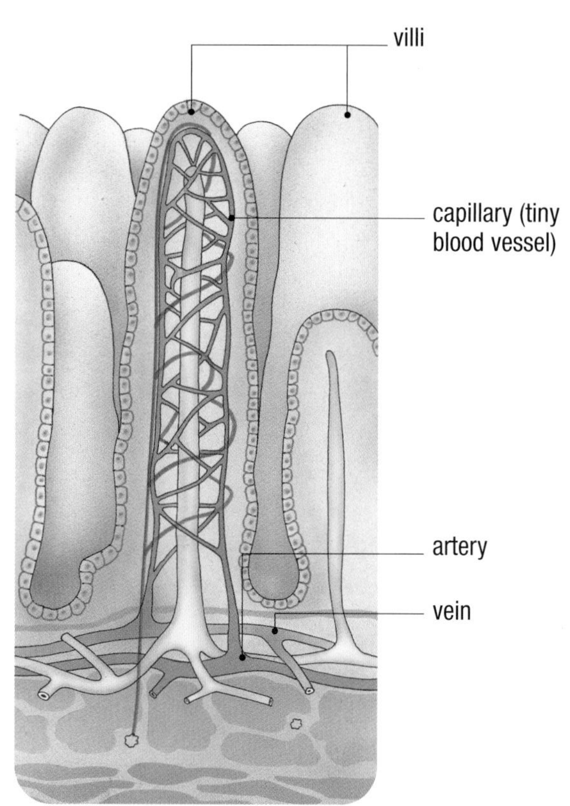

The inner layer of the small intestine is lined with millions of **villi**. Villi increase the surface area of the small intestine. As a result, more nutrients from digested food can be absorbed into the blood.

Waste food

Undigested food, such as the fibers from vegetables, passes into the large intestine. The large intestine absorbs water and more nutrients. Many helpful **bacteria**, called gut flora, live in the large intestine. They break down fiber, releasing nutrients and some **vitamins**. From the large intestine, the undigestable remains of the food, along with dead gut flora, passes through the anus and out of the body as feces.

CHAPTER 6

Chemical Messengers

The body often uses chemicals called **hormones** to send messages around the body. It takes a fraction of a second for electrical signals to pass along nerves. Hormones take much longer to have an effect. Hormones control many different body processes. They include growth and development, metabolism, and reproduction.

Hormones are made by organs called glands, which are found all over the body. Different glands make different hormones. They release the hormones directly into the bloodstream. In this way, the hormones can reach all the cells and tissues in the body. All the body's glands, and the hormones that they produce, make up the endocrine system. The hypothalamus is a tiny area in the middle of the brain. The hypothalamus is the control center of the endocrine system.

The body contains everything it needs to grow and develop from a baby into an adult. This information is programmed in our genes. Genes tell the body when to make certain hormones. For example, genes tell the body to produce special sex hormones. This marks the start of puberty, when a child's body slowly changes into the body of an adult.

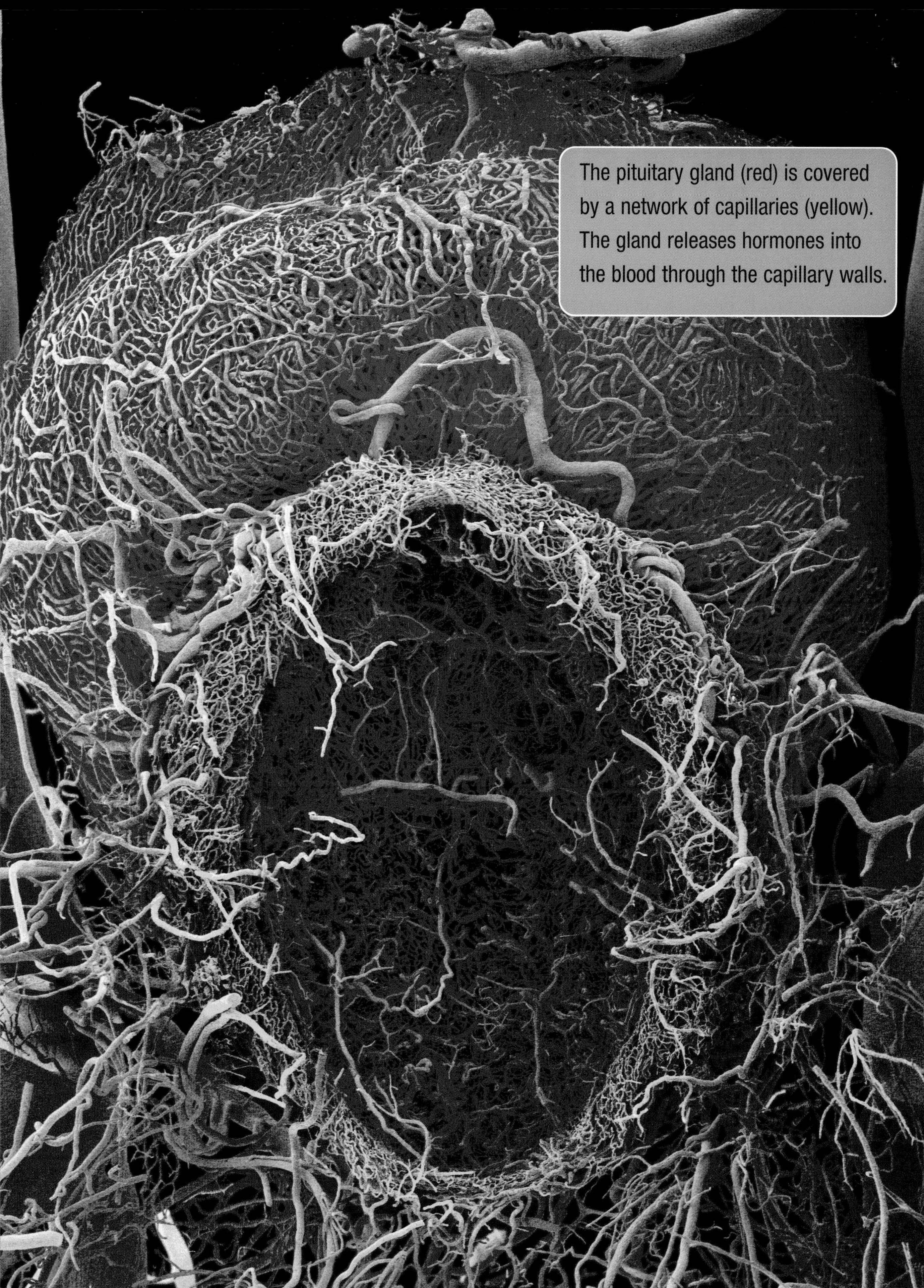

The pituitary gland (red) is covered by a network of capillaries (yellow). The gland releases hormones into the blood through the capillary walls.

Hormone Factories

The pituitary gland is the "master gland" because it controls many other glands in the body. It makes a hormone that stimulates the skin to darken in sunlight. It releases growth hormone, which helps to build and repair tissues all over the body. Growth hormone is especially important in children. The pituitary gland also releases hormones that bring about childbirth and also to make milk when the baby is born.

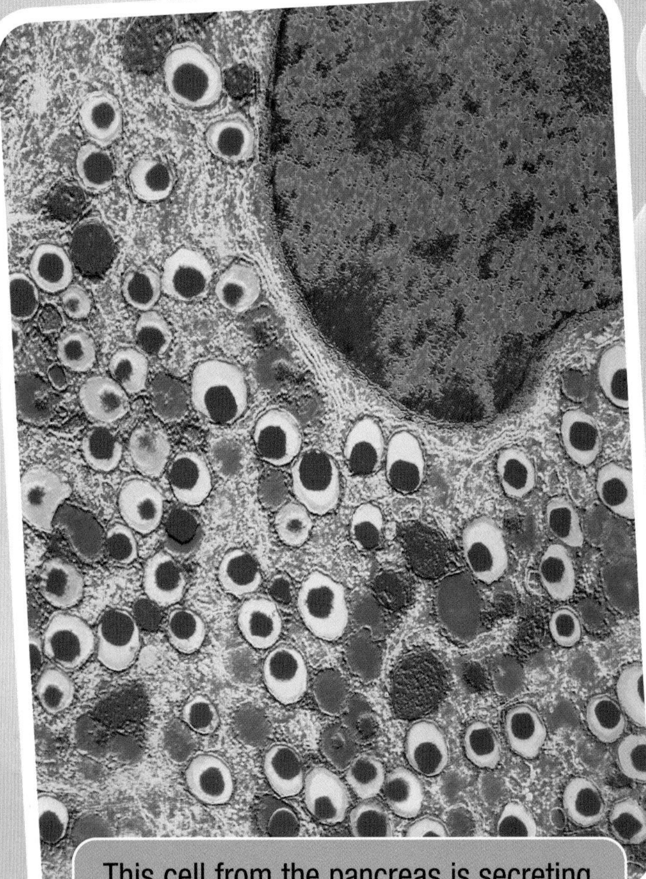

This cell from the pancreas is secreting hormones (red) to control the level of sugar in the blood.

The pancreas

In addition to making digestive enzymes, which help to break down food in the intestines, the pancreas makes three main hormones. They are made in groups of cells called islets of Langerhans. There are about one million islets in the pancreas. Some of these cells make the hormone glucagon, which is released when there is not enough sugar in the blood. Other cells make insulin, which lowers sugar levels when there is too much sugar in the blood. A third hormone, called somatostatin, controls the cells that produce glucagon and insulin. All three hormones work to ensure there is enough sugar in the blood.

Thyroid gland

The thyroid gland lies at the base of the neck, where it wraps around the top of the trachea. The thyroid makes two hormones—calcitonin and thyroxine. Calcitonin controls the amount of the mineral calcium in the blood and helps to keep all the bones of the skeleton strong. Thyroxine controls all the different chemical reactions that are going on inside the body. Some people do not make enough thyroxine. They become tired very easily and may gain a lot of weight. Others make too much and are overactive and may lose too much weight.

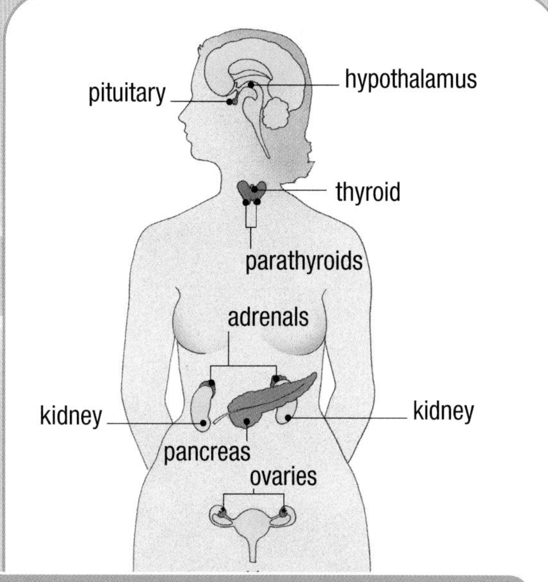

This artwork shows the main hormone-producing parts of a woman's body. Men have testes instead of ovaries as part of their reproductive systems.

Hormones work like a lock and key. The hormone (the key) fits into a receptor (the lock) on the cells of the target tissues. Different cells have different receptors so the hormones target only certain cells.

Reproduction

When it is ready, the body makes sex hormones. This starts the process of puberty, when a child becomes an adult who can have his or her own children. Girls and boys have different sex hormones. In girls, the main sex hormones are estrogen and progesterone. In boys, testosterone is the main sex hormone. Sex hormones act on the sex organs—male testes and female ovaries—so people can reproduce.

CHAPTER 7

Feeling Sick

Many different diseases, or illnesses, can make people feel very sick. Most people get ill many times during their lives. Some of these illnesses, such as the common cold and food poisoning, do not last for long, and usually they are not too serious. Others, such as certain types of cancers, can make people very sick.

Whenever someone is ill, it is important to see a doctor or another medical expert. They are trained to spot the signs of disease and help people get better. Many diseases and illnesses are easy to spot. Common colds usually come with a runny nose, a cough, high fever, and a sore throat. In some diseases, the signs are not obvious. The doctor might carry out more tests. For example, a doctor might check the chemical makeup of the blood. High or low levels of certain chemicals may reveal signs of organ damage. Samples of cells and tissues can also be taken and studied under a microscope to reveal the disease.

Once a doctor knows what is wrong, he or she can decide on the best course of treatment. Many illnesses can be cured with medication. Serious conditions may need surgery.

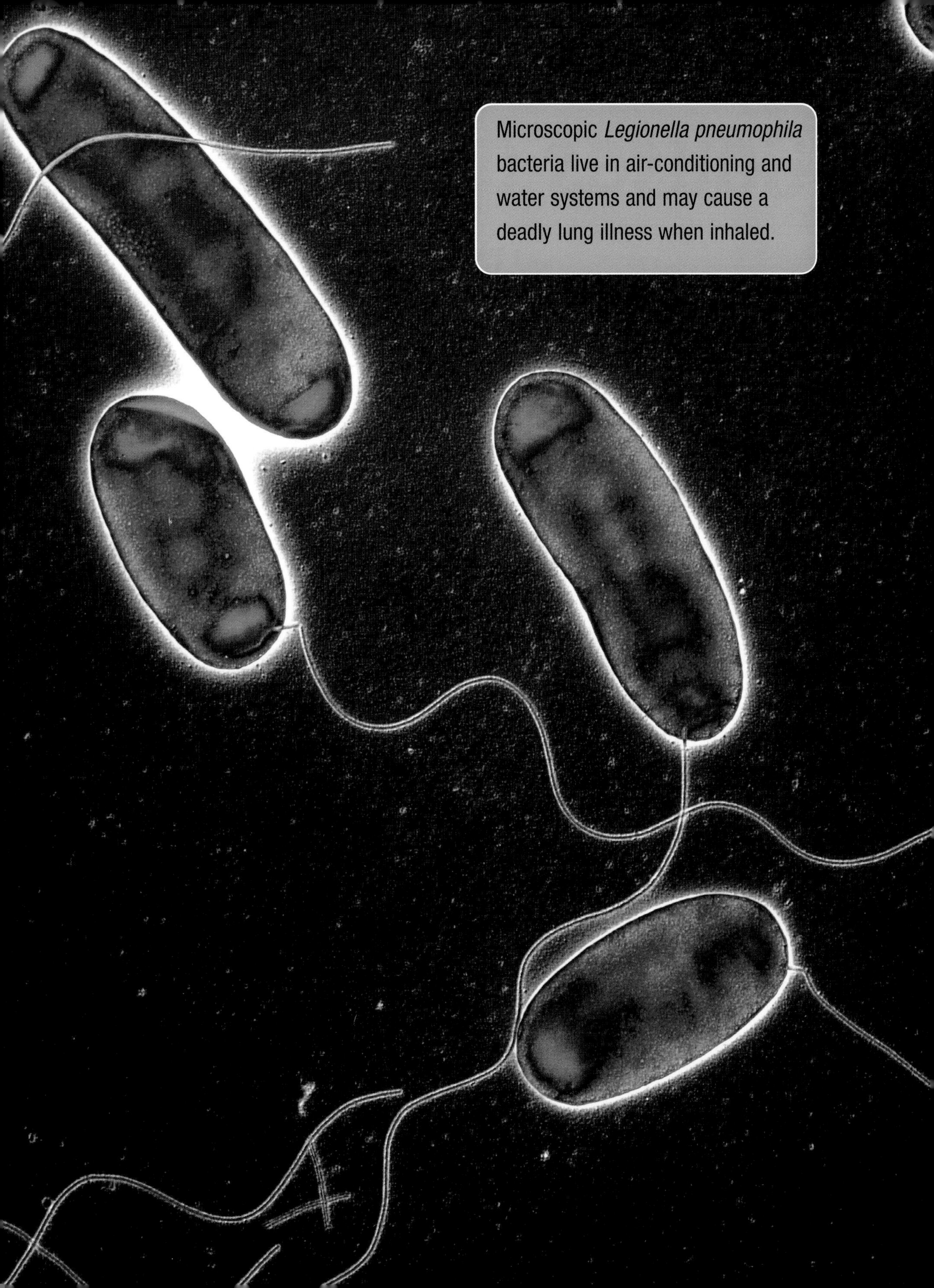

Microscopic *Legionella pneumophila* bacteria live in air-conditioning and water systems and may cause a deadly lung illness when inhaled.

Causes of Disease

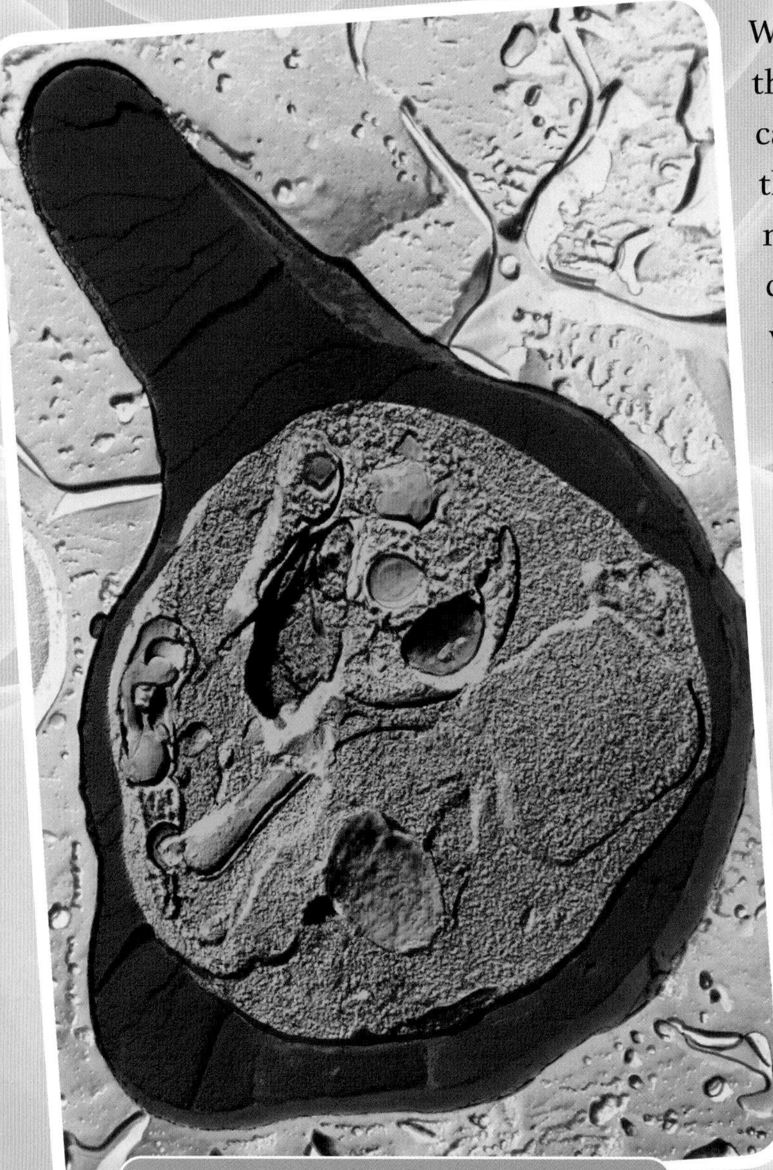

A malaria parasite (green) has infected a red blood cell. It is ready to burst out and infect other red blood cells.

When harmful germs get inside the body, they can multiply and cause infections. Germs invade the body through the mouth, nose, or cuts in the skin. The common cold is caused by a **virus** that is usually passed on when someone breathes in virus particles spread when infected people cough and sneeze.

Some infections are serious, and people can die from them. Malaria is a tropical fever caused by a single-celled parasite called a protozoan. Mosquitoes that carry the parasite pass it onto people when the mosquitoes bite. The most severe form of malaria produces a fever that kills millions of people each year in tropical countries.

Common diseases

In Western countries, people are most at risk of diabetes, heart disease, strokes, and cancer.

People with diabetes cannot use the sugars in food to make energy because the body does not have the right amounts of insulin. Too much or too little sugar in the blood can cause major health problems.

Heart disease and strokes occur when blood vessels become blocked by blood clots and fat deposits. When blood flow to the heart stops, a person may have a heart attack. Strokes occur when a clot or burst blood vessel means that oxygen cannot reach part of the brain.

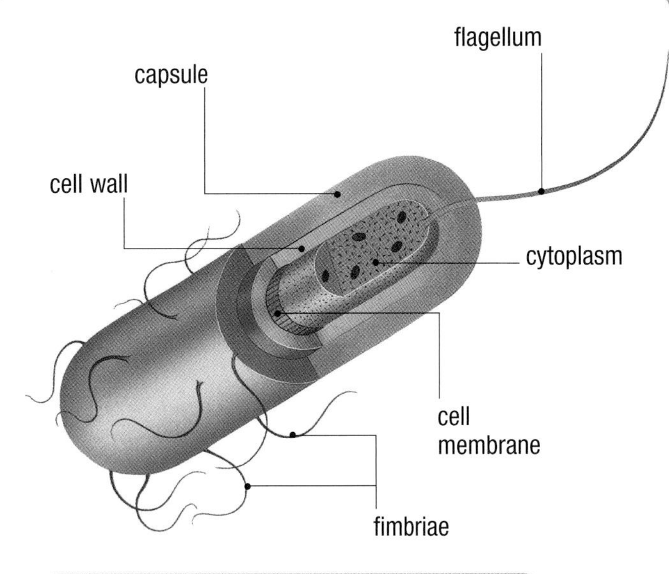

Most bacteria are enclosed within a cell membrane and surrounded by a cell wall. Some have a whiplike flagellum to move about and tiny fimbriae to grip to surfaces.

Cancers occur when body cells grow and divide too rapidly, forming a mass of tissue called a **tumor**. Cancer cells can spread to other parts of the body, where they grow into new tumors.

Tumors are bad because they steal nutrients, disrupt body processes, and damage cells and organs.

Genetic disorders

Many diseases run in families. If a parent has the disease, his or her children might be at risk, too. These kinds of diseases are called genetic disorders. Doctors are finding that more and more diseases are programmed in our genes.

Fighting Disease

When the signs of disease are not obvious, a doctor will look inside the body to find out what is wrong.

X rays are routine for broken or fractured bones. To see softer, hollow organs and tissues, doctors may ask for a contrast X ray. In this procedure, the patient drinks a liquid that contains a metal called barium. Barium blocks X rays in the same way that bone does, so the tissues or organs containing the barium will appear white on an X ray. Contrast X rays can reveal problems such as growths in the wall of the intestines.

CT scans and MRI can reveal problems that X rays cannot detect. Positron emission tomography (PET) scans show the organs as they are working in the body. PET scans are useful for detecting diseases of the brain. If X rays and scans do not work, a doctor can take samples of affected tissues or cells, or do surgery to look for signs of disease.

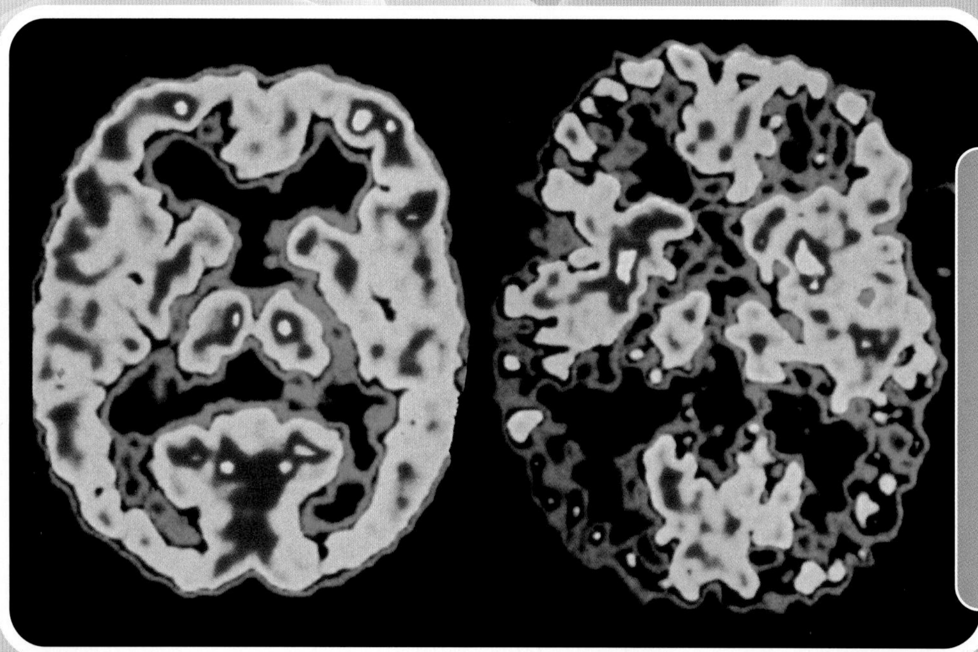

These PET scans show the brain of a healthy person (left) and the brain of a person with Alzheimer's disease (right). Alzheimer's disease affects brain matter and function.

Did You Know?

The body has a natural defense called the immune system to kill harmful germs before they cause disease. But some diseases, such as human immunodeficiency virus (HIV), attack the immune system so it cannot fight the disease.

Surgery

In some cases, surgery can treat a disease. Most surgery is now routine thanks to developments such as general anesthetics, which make people unconscious so they cannot feel pain. Technology such as the heart-lung machine keeps people alive during surgery on the heart.

Drugs and disease

Many germs infect billions of people every year. In the last century, better hygiene and medical treatment have wiped out many diseases. Today, drugs called antibiotics can cure illnesses that were once fatal.

Conclusion

Your body is an amazing living machine. The invisible world of the cell is the driving force behind that machine. Cells direct all the chemical reactions going on inside your body. These processes help the body keep on working every hour of every day—even at night when you are asleep. They keep your heart beating and muscles moving. They help you see, hear, and make sense of the world. They also help you fight off germs and stay healthy.

Today, scientists use powerful microscopes to delve deeper inside cells. They can see the nucleus inside cells and even the genes in the nucleus. They now know that genes provide the instructions for life. Genes determine how tall you will be, the color of your eyes—even your chance of developing a disease.

Scientists continue to explore the hidden world of the cell. They have already made some extraordinary discoveries. Who knows what the future holds in store?

Glossary

Alveoli Tiny air sacs, called alveoli, are found deep in the lungs.

Arteries These vessels carry blood away from the heart.

Axon The axon is the long threadlike part of a neuron.

Bacteria Bacteria are microscopic living things that often cause harmful diseases.

Bile This substance helps to break down fats in the body.

Capillaries These tiny blood vessels connect arteries and veins.

Carbohydrates These sugars are made up of the elements carbon, hydrogen, and oxygen.

Cartilage Tough tissue called cartilage is attached to the ends of bones.

Cells The smallest units of the human body are called cells.

Dendrites Spiky projections, called dendrites, bind neurons to nerve fibers.

Enzyme An enzyme is a protein that speeds up the chemical reactions inside the body.

Genes Instructions called genes inside the nuclei of cells tell the body what to do.

Hemoglobin A chemical called hemoglobin carries oxygen in red blood cells.

Hormone A hormone is a chemical that sends messages around the body in the blood.

Ligaments These tough tissues join bones to other bones.

Micron One micron is one millionth of a meter.

Neurons Individual nerve cells are called neurons.

Nutrients People need nutrients to grow and stay healthy.

Organelles Tiny objects, called organelles, do different jobs inside cells.

Organs Organs are groups of tissues that do a similar job.

Osteons Rod-shaped cells called osteons make up compact bone.

Peristalsis Peristalsis is the name given to the muscular contractions of the esophagus.

Proteins Substances called proteins help to build the body.

Retina The retina is the light-sensitive tissue inside the eye.

Synapse A synapse is a gap between two nerves.

Tissues Tissues are groups of cells that do similar jobs.

Tumor A tumor is a mass of cancer cells growing in the body.

Veins These vessels carry blood to the heart.

Villi Tiny projections, called villi, line the small intestines.

Virus A virus is a tiny particle that often causes disease.

Vitamins People need to eat vitamins to stay healthy.

Find Out More

Books

Cassan, Adolfo. *Introduction to the Human Body.* New York: Chelsea House Publications, 2005.

Gray, Leon, and John Woodward. *Our Bodies.* London: Brown Bear Books, 2007.

Spilsbury, Richard. *Cells, Tissues, and Organs.* Portsmouth, New Hampshire: Heinemann, 2008.

Taylor, Barbara. *The Best Book of the Human Body.* Boston: Kingfisher, 2008.

Walker, Richard. *How the Incredible Human Body Works... By the Brainwaves.* New York: DK Children, 2007.

Websites

http://www.bbc.co.uk/science/humanbody
The BBC website includes an interactive feature that allows you to build a skeleton and arrange the organs of the human body.

http://www.kidshealth.org/misc_pages/mybody_LP.html
This website for children includes a collection of illustrated articles that provide an in-depth look at the human body.

http://www.innerbody.com/htm/body.html
Take a tour of of all the major body systems at this website for students. Interactive diagrams help you identify the different body parts.

http://www.madsci.org/~lynn/VH
This website includes images and animations from the Visible Human Project at the Washington University Medical School.

Index

Page numbers in **boldface** are illustrations.